DANCE, PIONEER, DANCE!

"Those that have kept the covenants and served their God, if they wish to exercise themselves in any way to rest their minds and tire their bodies, go and enjoy yourselves in the dance, and let God be in all your thoughts in this as in all other things, and he will bless you."

—BRIGHAM YOUNG

DISCOURSES OF BRIGHAM YOUNG, p. 242

For my great-great pioneer grandparents—RW

For my mother, Claudia Teare—BT

Library of Congress Cataloging-in-Publication Data

Walton, Rick.
Dance, pioneer, dance! / by Rick Walton and Brad Teare.
p.   cm.
Summary: Pioneers and animals join in the dancing and the fun
during a journey across the plains.
ISBN 1-57345-243-2 (hb)
1. Frontier and pioneer life—West (U.S.)—Juvenile poetry.
2. Children's poetry, American.   [1. Frontier and pioneer life—
West (U.S.)—Poetry. 2. West (U.S.)—Poetry. 3. American poetry.]
I. Teare, Brad, 1956–   . II. Title.
PS3573.A4737D36   1997
811'.54—dc21   97-16451
                                                                             CIP
                                                                              AC

Printed in Mexico   18961
10   9   8   7   6   5   4   3   2   1

DANCE, PIONEER, DANCE!

Written by Rick Walton

Illustrated by Brad Teare

DESERET BOOK COMPANY

Salt Lake City, Utah

It's Friday night on the prairie.
The pioneers feel like dancing.
The fiddler tunes his fiddle.
The animals and people gather.
And Brigham Young begins . . .

Wagons pushin' hard all day.
Now it's time for us to play.
Grab a partner, hold on tight.
What d'you say? We'll dance tonight!

Hear the fiddler scratch that bow.
Grab a partner, off you go.
Shake those legs out, now's your chance.
Tap that toe and . . .

Pioneer, dance.
Pioneer, dance.
Pick up your heels and hitch up your pants.
Dance around the prairie.
Everyone be merry.
Dance, Pioneer, dance!

Right and left grand, away you fly
To the Valley by and by.
A right and left around the ring
While chickens fly and roosters sing.

Hand over hand around the square.
Stop and dance with the grizzly bear.
Kick those feet up, that's the trick.
Make 'em stare and . . .

Pioneer, kick.
  Pioneer, kick.
    Do it high and do it quick.
      Dance around the prairie.
    Everyone be merry.
  Kick, Pioneer, kick!

Toe, heel,
    How d'you feel?
        Listen to the piglets squeal.

Heel, toe,
    Away we go.
        Watch out for the buffalo.

Now swing that goat, don't be afraid.
Take that goat and promenade.
Horses stomp and cows be merry.
Promenade around the prairie.

Bow to your left,
Then bow to your right.
Swing that lizard, she won't bite.
Spin that cow, that pretty lil' thing.
Hold on tight and . . .

Pioneer, swing.
Pioneer, swing.
Hold on to that chicken wing.
Dance around the prairie.
Everyone be merry.
Swing, Pioneer, swing!

Now allemande left,
 away you fly.
  Grab that pony,
   pull her by.
    Grab that pony,
     dance all night
While the sky is clear and bright.

Now stop and jump! Jump all around.
Get those two feet off the ground.
Leap all night and never stop.
Go for height and . . .

Pioneer, hop.
Pioneer, hop.
Keep on leaping, hit the top.
Dance around the prairie.
Everyone be merry.
Hop, Pioneer, hop!

Ingo, bingo, sixpenny high,
Big pig, little pig, root hog or die!

Clara, Ellen, pirouette.
And don't forget
       Harriet.

Here we go with the covered wagon,
Hind wheel broke and the axle draggin'.
Dust in our eyes and dust in our hair.
Don't be laggin', we'll get there.

All join paws and head on west.
Ezra, Heber, dance your best.
On to Zion now, advance!
With the rest now . . .

Pioneer, dance.
Pioneer, dance.
Pick up your heels and hitch up your pants.
Dance across the prairie.
Everyone be merry.
Dance, Pioneer, dance!

THE CHARACTERS IN THIS STORY . . .

. . . really existed. They were members of the first party of Mormon pioneers to cross the plains. The party consisted of 143 men, 3 women, and 2 children. They left Winter Quarters in April, 1847, and arrived in the Valley of the Great Salt Lake on July 24, 1847.

Brigham Young led the Saints across the plains. Clara, Ellen, and Harriet were the three women in the party. Clarissa (Clara) Decker Young was the wife of Brigham Young. Ellen Sanders Kimball was married to Heber C. Kimball. Harriet Page Wheeler Young was Lorenzo Young's wife. (She was also Clarissa's mother.) Ezra and Heber were the apostles Ezra T. Benson and Heber C. Kimball, both ancestors of modern Latter-day Saint prophets.

The animals in this story really existed too. When the pioneers left Winter Quarters, they brought with them 93 horses, 66 oxen, 52 mules, 19 cows, 17 dogs, and some chickens. Along the way they also met plenty of other animals, including buffalo, wolves, owls, deer, antelope, rabbits, geese, wild turkeys, rattlesnakes, and prairie dogs. And probably even a pig or two.